Choices:

The Good

The Bad

The Ugly

Paula Abbott

For copies of this book or to book Paula Abbot for
your event or church, please contact:
Paula Abbott
P.O. Box 515
Terrell, TX 75160
469-595-6630
paula@roundpenministries.org

ISBN 978-1-937862-21-3

This book was published by BookCrafters,
Joe and Jan McDaniel SAN-859-6352
http://bookcrafters.net
http://self-publish-your-book.com
bookcrafters@comcast.net

Printed in the United States of America
by Snowfall Press.

Book edited by Tassie Winters in Kaufman, Texas
and Debbie with Anchor Printing in Terrell, Texas

Dedication

First and foremost, I want to dedicate this book to my Lord Jesus Christ for His unconditional Love and Grace. This is my story about how I met Jesus. At my deepest hour, down in Texas, wearing my boots and jeans, He walked into my life and changed me from the inside out. What a wonderful story of true redemption and awesome grace.

I would also like to thank my wonderful husband, Toby Abbott, for sharing with me the best years of my life. Through Toby, I have seen a personal example that nothing is unforgiveable and there is a peace that surpasses all in life just for me. Thank you, my love, for saddling up beside me on this journey of a lifetime. With your help, I have discovered that life can be enjoyed and not feared because with God all things are truly possible for those who believe. Thank you, Mother for standing strong and loving me through all the storms in my life. And finally, a big thank you to my brother, Jerry, for being my best friend and always being there for me to talk to.

Table of Contents

About the Author

Paula Abbott was born and raised in West Texas. She is a Texas girl through and through. Being around cattle and horses her whole life placed a love for the western culture deep down inside her soul. In 1999, Paula met and married a cowboy from Amarillo, Texas, Toby Abbott. Paula is a mother of three grown children, two teenage step-children and two beautiful granddaughters.

Paula Abbott was ordained in 2004 and is the associate Pastor of a Cowboy Church just east of Dallas, Texas. She also serves as an inspirational speaker to people all over the United States by delivering a powerful and life changing message about living a victorious life in Christ Jesus. She has connected with audiences abroad about difficult subjects including drug and alcohol addiction, personal rejection, physical and emotional abuse. God has led her to share her sermons with people in various life stages in multiple facets Nationwide. She shares God's message with hungry hearts who are willing to listen, receive, and allow God to deliver an amazing, life-changing transformation. Her messages are powerful, full of energy and very exciting.

Chapter 1
The Great John Wayne

I was raised up loving the great and mighty John Wayne. I guess most of you know who John Wayne is, right? John Wayne's movies always had a great ending, didn't they? He was always "the hero." As a little girl there wasn't much to watch on T.V., maybe only three channels if the wind wasn't blowing. So, it was a real treat when a John Wayne movie was on the T.V.

I remember sitting in front of the T.V. with a bowl of Captain Crunch, watching John Wayne dominate the Wild West and becoming the hero, conquering and capturing all the bad guys.

As I reflect back on those "wild-west" days, I see a place where good people really did win in the end. I remember that I always wanted to ride off in the sunset like he did knowing that everything was going to be okay and that if you did what was right because it was right then good would always win in the end.

You know T.V. back then was nothing like it is today. Nowadays most of us have over 300 channels available in our homes, and video stores are just around the corner. Today, we can watch just about any movie with a point and click of a remote control. Movies just don't have that special meaning like they did back in my day.

When a good movie was going to be on T.V., my family would make plans to watch it together because it may be another year or so before it came on again. And, going to the movies just wasn't my father's style. So T.V. was about it for me.

The Wild West, it was a real place in my heart. It was a place where I could escape when I was a little girl, even if it was only a dream. I could always ride off into the sunset after winning the battle over the bad guys.

You know, I was always told that when you quit dreaming, then you've stopped living. Well, today I have a story to tell you about a real life hero who personally touched my life. No, it was not John Wayne.

It wasn't in the Wild, Wild, West, but it is about my life, and it was Wild and totally out of control until a man named Jesus Christ came to the rescue during what I have come to know as my deepest hour.

Chapter 2
The Pearls

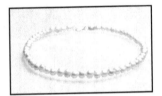

There once was a little girl that went shopping with her mother. Already a good story huh? Just the word shopping can get our attention. Shopping now that's the ticket, you can count me in. Okay, enough of that, we have too little time and too little money; let's get back to the story. They were shopping at the dime store when the little girl spotted a small pink box. This little pink box really caught her eye and as she got closer, she noticed a pearl necklace inside.

Her desire for the pearl necklace grew stronger and stronger as she stood there looking at it. Now notice that the word desire is a very powerful word.

It means to "long for, to wish for, a craving for or something that brings satisfaction and enjoyment."

Well, the little girl called for her mother to come and see the pretty pink box that held the dime store set of pearls. Her mother picked up the box and found the price, which was only a $1.99. She told the little girl that she would have to save up her money so she could buy the necklace for herself. The mother knew that if the little girl saved the money for herself that she would take better care of the necklace.

The little girl was so excited that she talked about how she was going to save for that necklace all the way home. The little girl's mother told her, "You'll have to do a few chores around the house to make some extra money. Your birthday is coming up and maybe your grandmother will give you a crisp one dollar bill."

The little girl went right to work doing chores around the house and then came her birthday. Just like her mother had told her, her grandmother gave her a crisp one dollar bill. She ran to her room and counted the money she had saved, and discovered she had exactly

$1.99. Knowing that the little girl had worked hard for this money, her mother took her back to the dime store, so she could purchase the pearl necklace for herself. The little girl was so proud of her necklace that she never took it off.

Now, let me remind you, this necklace was a dime store necklace it was not the real thing. But this little girl loved her necklace so much that she kept the necklace on day after day - bath after bath - until it began to turn her neck green.

I do believe that most of us have worn something like this in our younger days. It could have been something like a ring, earrings, or a necklace. They really look great at first, but in time they start to show their "true" colors. Well, her father took notice of the green around the little girl's neck and began to plan a way to get the necklace away from her. Knowing that it was not going to be easy he prayed for God to give him wisdom and knowledge.

The little girl's father always read a bedtime story to her every night before she went to sleep. One night, as he walked into her room, he asked her if she would give him the necklace. With weeping and crying the little girl said, "No Daddy! No Daddy! Please not my necklace. Please Daddy, don't take my necklace. You can have anything else, but not the necklace."

Seeing that she was not going to give him the necklace that easily, her father went on to read her the story and then kissed her good night. The next night her father came in for the bedtime story, but first he asked her if she would give him her necklace.

Again, the little girl began to weep and cry, saying "Please Daddy! Please Daddy! Don't take my necklace. You can take anything else, "Anything else, but not my necklace." This went on for weeks with her father knowing that the fake necklace was destroying her appearance and the smell it left was getting worse.

He knew that to help his little girl, it had to be her "choice" to give it up. Then finally one night as the father came into her room he saw his daughter sitting on the edge of her bed holding something tightly in her hand. With tears running down her face, she held out her hand and said, "It's time Daddy, it's time. You can have my necklace now." With deep compassion her father reached out and took the worn out fake necklace from her hand and then embraced her.

With a tear in his eyes, he cleaned the green smelly icky ring away from her neck that the "Fake Pearls" had left. At that moment, he then took a beautiful blue velvet bag from his pocket and opened it. Inside was a "Real" set of pearls. With this set of pearls she could wear them everyday and through every bath. These pearls were the real thing, promising never to turn her neck green or to destroy her appearance again.

She was so excited that her tears immediately stopped. The father then placed on her neck the set of "Real Pearls," ones that would never turn her neck green. The little girl had just made the trade from something fake to something real. You see she had to make that "choice" for herself to receive the real set of pearls. The choice had to come from her and not her father.

I share this story of the pearls with you today because all in all I am that little girl. The necklace was my life; I lived a fake life for so long that it was starting to turn my spirit and soul green from poison.

Many times, I was asked to trade the way I was living for a life that was real. You see my life was fake and taking over the reality of everyday living. For many years, I could not let go of the life I knew. I struggled for years with doing things my way, versus the "right way." With my life spinning out of control, it was time for me to "Make the Trade" from a life of pain to a life of peace.

I had "Choices" to make and needed to make them soon. This is my story, on how I found Victory through Jesus Christ in my "Boots-n-Jeans" in a Cowboy Church just on the outskirts of Amarillo, Texas.

Chapter 3
In The Beginning

I was born an unwanted child, to a woman that had major problems in her own life. She did not know who my father was and she had no desire to raise me. She ran off and left me at the age of 6 months. My mother had been staying with a man she had met during her pregnancy. He was "a stranger." I was left at the house of this man who was not my father. I was left in the arms of a stranger. Not knowing how to handle all this, this man took me to his brother's and his wife's home, while he went to work. That day he was killed. Left again I begin to feel unwanted and unworthy. I felt like there was something wrong with me. I was a cute baby, why in the world would someone want to leave me and not come back?

Those questions have haunted me my whole life. What did I do to make my mom want to leave? As an adult, reflecting on my childhood, I began to form this perception of myself that no one must have wanted me. I know that I must have been screaming out with all my heart, "Please someone take the baby." Didn't anyone know that my spirit was hurting? I had done nothing wrong, why didn't someone want me? I started to feel a huge void inside my spirit.

Finally, at the age of eight months, I was adopted by a woman that really wanted children with all her heart. She was not able to have children and having a little girl would be a wonderful addition to her family, but her husband did not want children and he did not share the same feelings.

Let me start by saying that this was not a Christian home – actually this was not a very happy home. My adopted father was an atheist and we were not allowed to go to church, nor did we ever speak of it. My adopted father was full of hate, anger and was a very abusive man.

He made it crystal clear that I was not wanted there. My new mother was a soft place to fall for me. She was the light in a dark place. Later in my adult life, she told me that I needed someone to hold me almost every minute of every day and night, out of fear that I would be left again. I know that this must have hurt my new parents and their relationship. My father was not loved as a child and he did not know how to love. You know the saying, "You can't give what you don't have?" Love was something that he did not feel nor show towards me or my new family. He made life miserable for me, my mother, and my older brother. You see they adopted another child, a boy who was eight years older than me. Oh, how I loved my new brother!

His name was Gerald Robert, but I called him Jerry. Our hearts grew together as if we were truly brother and sister. He loved me and disliked me all at the same time. You know, how little sisters could be. I could write a whole book on the adventures my brother and I took, but let's talk about my father and the root cause of my out of control life. My father was a powerful and rich man. He thought that he could buy anything, including the love of his family. Money was something he had - love on the other hand was something he did not have.

I was told that he never experienced the love of a family. I never heard much about his father, but I was told that his mother was mean and abusive to him his whole life. My father, at the age of 13, was so abused that he ran away from home and was living on his own at the local feed yard. I was told that he worked cattle for his room and board. This was the life he grew into as a young business man.

My father became a very successful cattleman and a very successful businessman in every way. In addition to the cattle business he owned nightclubs, a horse race track and bail bond companies. He overcame the odds that began in his younger life and proved to the world that he would be a person of control and authority. That no one would ever control him again. My father was successful with everything, but his family. Sometimes my mother was just one of his hired hands. As a young girl, I never saw any passion between my mom and dad and for that my heart hurts for my mother. My mother did the best that she could to make our family whole and to make my father happy.

My mom was strong, yet soft when it came to loving me. Let me start by saying that my out-of-control life is not my Father's fault, it was mine. I had to accept the things I did, but I also found the root of my problems were birthed as a result of the rejection and emotional abuse from my father.

Chapter 4
The Rejection

By the time I was four or five, I wanted so much for my father to love and accept me, that I would do anything to receive his approval. I would be the best little girl any father could ever ask for. I wanted his attention so badly that I would do anything to get it. I tried so hard to please him. But, remember, this man didn't even want children. He was living the fast life and family had no place in it. He was rarely home, but when he was I spent most of my time trying to fit into his world.

I would catch my mother crying most of the time, which in turn would make me cry. Didn't know why we were crying, but if she was unhappy then so was I. My father was very mentally and emotionally abusive. His words were always harsh and full of hate. They were sharp and could cut deep into your soul and spirit.

Do you remember that ol' saying when we were kids, "Sticks and Stones may break my bones, but words will never hurt me?" As children, when someone said something mean and hurtful to us, we would always come back with this phrase. How funny that we actually thought this phrase could shield us from the effects of hurtful words.

This phrase is not true! It is so far from the truth. Who ever made up that phrase did not know my father and how painful the words were to my spirit and emotions. You know, broken bones will heal in time, but a broken spirit can and often does last a lifetime. I was broken deep down inside and it wasn't getting better anytime soon.

I was told by my father that I was worthless and would never amount to anything. He told me that everything I did was wrong. It wasn't good enough for him. I thought if I could just be a better person, then maybe he would love me. Basically, at a very young age, I began to feel like I was worthless and that I would do nothing right.

My mother worked hard on giving me everything I needed and wanted, but it was because of the rejection of my father I felt worthless. Have you heard the ol' saying, "We want what we can't have?" Well, I never had a relationship with my father and that's what I wanted. Every time he would come home I would catch myself fighting for his attention, only to be rejected once again.

So feeling unwanted and worthless from my father, I tried to take my life at the age of seven. That's right, seven years old. Isn't that the craziest thing you have ever heard?

My mother took me to the hospital and of course my father stayed at home to watch some T.V. You see, he had worked a really long day and was tired. A trip to the hospital was not in his plans for that evening. So alone, scared, and panicked my mother drove me to the hospital. She needed the support of my father and did not receive it, just like many times before.

Let me ask you a question. How many of you have children or grandchildren that are around the age of seven? You would never think that a seven year old could even think of something like that. I should have had other things on my mind, like puppies, friends, playing ball, school, and yes even homework, but instead all I had on my mind was receiving the approval and the attention of my Father. This started something called "Approval Addiction" in my life. I had a huge void deep down inside my spirit, and needed to fill it.

When we are born, we are born into a natural body made up of three (3) parts; body, soul and spirit. The body contains our five senses; taste, touch, smell, sight and hearing. Our soul is our mind, feelings, and emotions. Then, we have our spirit. Our spirit is created for one thing and one thing only and that is to glorify God. Before we receive Jesus Christ as our Lord and Savior our spirit is dead. I tried filling my spirit with my earthly father and it never worked. That's why his rejection was controlling my life. Remember we did not go to Church, so I did not know who Jesus was, so therefore my spirit was dead and empty.

My mom brought me home from the hospital and I gave her the note I had written to my father and left on my bed. In that note, I told him that all I wanted was his love and if I couldn't have it, I didn't want to live. I'm not sure what happened when she told him or showed him the note. All I know is that I saw her go to the kitchen and could hear her crying. Things did not change for me and my father, so I became addicted to seeking his approval and love once again. My life had become a life of what I now call, "Approval Addiction."

Chapter 5
My Pony "Nubbins"

Whenⁿ I went to school, I would do anything for the approval of others, even if it meant doing stupid stuff. Have any of you found yourselves acting stupid to just try and fit in with the crowd? Well, that was me - stupid and trying to fit in.

You see, I didn't have many friends. Not many people wanted to come to my house because of my father. Everyone in the town knew how mean he was. So friends were really out of the question. I ended up becoming a loner. I played by myself much of the time.

My brother was eight years older than I was and he had different things on his mind than playing with his younger sister. That's where my love for animals was birthed and it grew stronger and stronger.

My father had a very successful cattle business and was gone 80% of the time. This business kept my mother busy day after day, so I would find myself out in the barn everyday talking to the horses, dogs, and cows. Pretty much talking to whoever or whatever would listen. It was easy talking with the animals, because they didn't judge me. They seem to always love me no matter what.

I was interested in sports, but due to the time it took for practices and games, I wasn't able to participate and that was okay with me. I didn't want to give my mom more to handle because her plate was so full as it was. So, I found myself riding horses and playing with the animals. My father owned a horse race track just back of our home in Lubbock, Texas and I would find myself down at the barns by that track just about everyday.

I had a small pony named "Nubbins" and I would dream that he was a famous race horse. Didn't matter to me that he was short and had a few bad habits. He was mine and I loved him so. He and I spent many hours down at the track. There's no telling what people thought when they saw us. But, I didn't care. I loved that horse and he was my friend, habits and all.

One day, he got the chance to show all those big time race horses who he really was. One Sunday, there was a race that ponies could ride in, and my brother Jerry rode Nubbins because I was not old enough. To everyone's surprise, Nubbins won first place! Of course, it didn't make my father happy. It was just another day to him. But to me, it was an awesome day. It took me away from the pain that I was feeling inside, if only for a moment. My little pony Nubbins was a thoroughbred and worth a million dollars to me. What a day I'll never forget.

Chapter 6
Mom and I Left Dad

Due to the mental abuse year after many years my mother left my father and my parents divorced when I was fifteen, and of course my father didn't want me or anything to do with me. My mother…well, let's just say she was fighting her own broken spirit during that time. She had been through twenty plus years of harsh, hateful, and abusive words from my father. She needed some time to heal from a seriously broken spirit and learn to live again.

So at the age of only sixteen, I found myself in another abusive relationship with an older man. Someone that I had just met inside a bar who gave me the attention I was seeking.

You see at the age of sixteen, I had quit school and started hanging out with the wrong crowd, made some bad decisions, and ended up in the bars. I was raped by this older man at the age of sixteen and by the time I was seventeen, I had a child with him.

Abuse had become a way of life it seemed. I thought that abuse was normal and didn't know anything different. That man was meaner than a junk yard dog. Drinking was his main interest and when he was drunk, he loved to fight and it didn't matter who was in the way, he just wanted to have a really good ol' brawl. Unfortunately, I was usually the one who was in the way at the wrong time. Unbelievable to me now, I married this man because we had a baby coming soon. We did not have a normal marriage at all. This marriage was maintained and lived through fear for three years.

Having sex with him was scary, painful, and harsh. He made me feel very dirty and ashamed. He would beat me during and after sex. Control was his game and he was very good at it. We had a calendar that hung on the wall with big red X's on it. The red X was to indicate the day he expected to have sex with me and I needed to be ready. It came to the point that when I knew that date was coming, I would just cover myself with the shield of warped thinking, repeating to myself, "I'm worthless, this is just who I am. This must be something that I deserve."

I lived three years with this man and he became so violent that it was only a matter of time before I knew he would begin to abuse our daughter. My cousins from out of state adopted her and I began to run. Running for my life because, he had become obsessed with wanting to kill me. You see like many women in similar situations, I had myself convinced that he would change. I was still looking for the "Father Figure" that I'd been seeking all of my life. I was still too young to know that you can't change someone who doesn't want to be changed.

Out of fear, I ran from him for many years. This man ended up marrying another woman a few years later and ended up being killed by that woman's son because he began to beat her too.

I thank God everyday that I left when I did, that could have been me or my child. I have never talked with his family, but since found out that many of them are all in prison. Just so you know, my beautiful daughter is doing wonderful. She is married to a great guy and they now live in California. I have been able to stay in close contact with her and she found a way to forgive me for letting her go. Today we have a close and flourishing friendship and I give God all the credit for making that possible.

Chapter 7
After the Split Up

After I left and my daughter was safe in another state, I began to run. I was running from nothing basically, just myself. You see my spirit was still dead. I had never been to Church or around anything that was positive. I had a huge void deep inside my spirit that I needed filled. I thought that I would fill it on my own, but I was wrong.

I ended up having two more children by my mid-twenties. No matter who I was with, I was never happy. I had a huge void in my life that no one could fill. I was trying to live a normal life, but didn't know how. I had two wonderful children, but for some reason I was never happy and that void inside me was never filled.

I was seeking something and I didn't know what it was. I couldn't give to my family what I never had. I didn't know how to love anyone because I have never had love shown to me. Recently, I read something that told me when you're not hugged and loved as a child, there's a part inside of you that has never had the chance to grow; therefore you never learn how to love anyone. I guess kinda like my father was and in truth that was me too. I didn't know how to give something I didn't have.

I was always finding myself alone and wishing my life was different. You see, I was living a fake life. I was going through all the motions with my family, but didn't really fit in.

I would remember what my father had told me when I was young. He told me that I was worthless and would never amount to anything. So I felt that I had nothing to offer to my husband or my children. I felt so worthless and unworthy that surely no one wanted me around. My spirit was so damaged that nothing could make it any better. No, not even the love and smiles of my two wonderful children.

Chapter 8
My trip to Kansas City

In my late twenties, I ended up in a night club listening to a Rock and Roll band. I was not into Rock and Roll, mostly just country, but this is where I ended up. I guess you could say I was looking for something dark and unknown. Kinda, like my life. A week later, I ended up following this band to their hometown, Kansas City. I ended up turning to drugs and alcohol to fill that void that I could not fill on my own. Leaving my children and my family behind, I had found my new "Love" - Meth was its name.

"Methamphetamine"

They asked me to go to a party with them just one time and see what I thought. I really didn't think twice, I thought that I was in control of everything and it was just a party. "I was in control. Right?"

Well, it was a party all right, a Methamphetamine party and the one time thing was over with, on my first hit. I was hooked! "Oh, now this was the answer to all my problems." Or, at least I thought it was. I was really only living a life that was fake; actually nothing about it was real. I had new friends, new boyfriends, pretty much new everything. I was the life of the party, which ended up being many parties, and before I knew it one thing led to another, and I found myself leading a life as a stripper.

The drugs were very expensive and I needed a quick way to make the money to buy them, so I used what I had, my body.

At this point in my life, it didn't seem to matter what happened to me. I found myself right in the middle of a big mess. I was engulfed by this new found life that I had. This is the part of the story that I call the Wild, Wild, West, because my life was out of control. I found myself in the deepest pit of my life and I was going down fast. Methamphetamine had become my best friend "morning, noon, and night."

In these bars I found the attention I was seeking and it started filling that void inside my spirit, even if it was only for a night, or so I thought at the time. I had no plans or goals for my life.

I was content just living day by day because having that drug in my system gave me the false sensation that I was invincible and would certainly live forever. I thought that I was really in control of my "out of control" life. I didn't have any type of goals or dreams in my life to motivate me. In reality, I was a "Dead" person walking. This was my life and I deserved it.

Chapter 9
The Deepest Pit in My Life

Even though I felt invincible, I still had a personal self image that I was and always would be a failure. I never thought that I could do anything, so I never tried. Instead, I just gave up. I was a quitter and a good one. I learned at a young age to "never believe in something that I could never have" and that something was my soul's greatest desire "Peace and Love." I always thought that I was worthless and I would never amount to anything. I found myself quitting everything before I ever got started.

In my mind, everything was temporary and nothing was real. I thought the parties were it, and I was always the center of attention. But you know something "the parties came to an end, they never went on forever."

The so called "friends," well they left, and then I was by myself again, feeling that huge void deep down inside. It was like an endless pit, the madness was never ending. This part of my life was out of control and very wild to say the least. For thirteen years, I was free falling into the deepest, darkest pit of my life. It was cold and dark and not known to many. I needed help and I needed it badly. I didn't know where to go and I didn't know how to get out of my pit. The walls were closing in fast. I couldn't breathe and I never saw the sunlight of day. The harder I tried to get out the pit, the faster I fell. There was no way out, or so I thought. During that thirteen year period, I tried two more times to take my life. I was done and didn't want to try anymore. As I think back on my suicidal attempts, I have discovered that I really never wanted to die I just wanted the pain to stop. I was crying out for help to whoever would listen.

I was always seeking something to fill that void that was deep down inside me. The drugs and alcohol would only last for a while and then the high they brought was gone too.

Nothing could fill that void in my life. Not the drugs, not the alcohol, not the men, and no amount of money. Honestly, I was broke, busted, and disgusted. I found myself in a place where I had no where to turn.

After the second attempt to take my life, I was placed in a mental institution because I had become a very real and dangerous threat to myself. I was locked up for weeks in a cold gray room located in the basement of a hospital in Kansas City. I was depressed and didn't want to live anymore. I had nothing to live for. I didn't feel anything in my heart or in my spirit. I was completely numb.

I didn't care what happened to me, I just needed a way out and I thought if I could end it, I would be in a better place. I was not able to take my life as long as I was locked up, so my last hope was to call my mom and see if she would come get me out.

So, I did. I called my mother for help, but she didn't know how to help me. Looking back on that phone call now, I realized that what she did was the best thing she had ever done for me, and that was by telling me "NO." She was starting her new life and didn't know how to deal with me and my lifestyle.

As I sat there thinking about this life I had wasted, I knew that I was missing something. I didn't know what it was, but I knew I was missing something big in life. The quiet solitude of that institution returned my emotional and spiritual emptiness that I had felt so many times before.

I realized that I didn't have any goals or purpose for my life, and I didn't have any "real" friends, but most of all I didn't have peace. It was either time to complete the task at hand or straighten up and fly right. So, I decided that I needed to straighten up and fly right or at least that's what I told them and to my surprise they let me go.

Chapter 10
Back Home to Texas

I went back home to Texas and moved in with my brother and tried to make a go at my life, but fell right back into the drug scene. I still didn't have the confidence or the strength that I needed to turn my life around, and I went back to my good old friend, "Methamphetamine," which gave me the confidence I thought I needed. You see, I had been told since a child that I would never amount to anything, and that's all I knew. That was just my life, and I quite simply I didn't know any better.

Then one night in Amarillo, Texas as I was driving to meet my drug dealer, I passed a sign on the side of the road that read, "Cowboy Church Saturday nights at 7:00pm." It was kinda like a revelation, someone screaming to me, "Paula, Here's Your Sign." This was a big sign with big red letters that read:

"COWBOY" CHURCH

Well, being the Cowgirl that I was, the "Cowboy" part of the sign caught my attention. I would have never noticed that sign if it only had of said "Church." I was not one of those church type people, and I was not going to have someone tell me that I was living in sin. You see, I had never really been to church and didn't know anything about church. I always thought they were kind of cultic and brain wash people into believing all kinds of strange things. But on the other hand, the sign did say "Cowboy Church," so I thought to myself, "This means there will be cowboys around." Now men; especially cowboys was something I could relate to or so I thought at that time.

You see, I was a honky-tonk, bar type of girl. I was raised up around cowboys and bars most all of my life. I loved rodeos and pretty much anything to do with "Cowboys." So, I thought to myself, it can't be so bad if there are really cowboys there, and since this "Cowboy Church" started at 7:00, I should be out of there by 8:00 and that would give me just enough time to make it to the bar. But, I didn't stop that night, I went on to meet the drug dealer and then out to the bar.

I did however, think about the Church again that next week and I decided to try it out that next Saturday before I went to the bar. But, little did I know what was in store for me that night.

Chapter 11
"COWBOY" CHURCH

Through that next week, I thought about that sign on the side of the road from time to time and wondered if I should go. I never knew too much about churches or even what the people in those kinds of places did, so this was new territory for me. You see I was a CEO Christian "Christmas and Easter Only." It was a bit of a struggle within myself to even have the mindset that I would try this kind of place out. Ultimately I thought, "Hey, I've always liked a challenge." So, I ended up visiting that next Saturday.

When I arrived, I was already high on my drugs and I had already enjoyed several drinks. I was a mess and that's very much an understatement. When I walked in, I was amazed that no one there made me feel uncomfortable. Instead, I got a warm "Howdy!" and a big hug.

Okay that kinda freaked me out a little. I just knew that they were going to suck my brains out and implant new thoughts into my head like some alien invasion or something. BUT - Bless God I'm not letting these "Church People" get to me. You know, I had to keep that wall up just in case they got too close.

You see, I thought that when you became a Christian that you would lose everything in your life; your brain, then your entire life including your truck, which may seem kind of juvenile to think about, but I'm a cowgirl and in my state of mind, if my truck was gone, you may as well take my life along with it. I was so afraid that I would have to start riding a bike, with a white shirt and tie and that I would have to carry Bibles around, knocking on doors talking about things I didn't really even understand.

As I stood there inside that church, I didn't feel so good. I was thinking all kinds of thoughts in my head. Just so you'll know, "I was not going to ride a bike and knock on doors." You are not going to get my brain and take my truck. With this kind of thinking, I had already formed a high wall around myself, before I ever walked in. But, I had noticed some good looking cowboys walking in and, well that took my mind somewhere else and so I decided to stay. I know what you're thinking, and yes it was only because of the cowboys that I stayed. I know that's wrong now, but at least I stayed. God, can and will use whatever He can to get our attention. And let me tell you, those cowboys were used in a completely different way that evening than they'd ever been used in a church atmosphere and they had every bit of my attention.

Well, they told me to make myself at home and if I needed anything, just to let them know. So, I went in and sat in the back so no one would know I was there. You know, I had only heard about this Jesus person around Christmas and Easter time, but I didn't really know who He was. I always thought that He was someone like Santa or maybe the Easter Bunny. I had no clue who He really was at all. I was pretty dumb in that area.

There was a man by the name of Glenn Smith there that night to preach. "Hey," I thought to myself, "I knew of this guy. He was a PRCA Cowboy, the real thing.

What in the world was he doing in a church? He was too tough to be in a church. Real cowboys didn't go to church. He was the real deal; boots, bucket, and big truck. Now, how did he get to keep his truck?" I thought, "He still looks like a real cowboy, so maybe this isn't going to be too bad after all."

Okay, I'm in the back of the room by myself taking all this in. Then, the music started and it was Country Christian music. I loved country music, which was something that I could relate to. Well, I thought to myself "the music wasn't too bad, so I guess I can sit through the rest." At that moment I caught my foot tapping to the beat. I looked down and said "Excuse me, we are not having fun here. What are you doing?"

Then here comes the preacher and I found myself sinking down in my seat so he wouldn't see me. Being the new person and all, I didn't want him to notice me and say something. As I listened, I realized that he wasn't one of those preachers that made you feel bad for things you've done. He actually was kinda funny and made me laugh. I hadn't really laughed in a while.

So, I begin to listen to him and caught myself understanding what he was saying. I could relate to him and where he had come from. It was as if he was talking straight to me that night. He talked a lot about this Jesus person and how to have that void in your life filled.

I got a little scared hearing all of this because I didn't tell anyone I was going to be at that Church that night and he knew way too much about me and my life. So, if I didn't tell him I'd be at church that night, who did? I starting thinking about the people I had talked to, to try and figure out who I might have told that could have let someone there know to expect me. You see, I needed to keep my image up and going to church, was not my style and if anyone found out - that was the end of my world, so I came to the conclusion that I hadn't told anyone. So, how did this guy know all about my life?

Well, I took all this Church talk in stride and didn't think too much of it. Because remember, I was keeping my guard up, you know against those "Church People." But, when I left that night something had happened to me, I had something planted in my heart. I didn't know what I was feeling, but it was different, that's for sure.

So, I went on my way and I came back from time to time to hear a little bit more about this Jesus person. You see, I was feeling something inside and wasn't sure what it was. I tried to just go on and live my life the way I always did, but something kept tugging at me. I believe that a seed was planted in my heart that night. Not even accepting it, it happened.

When I was at the bars or parties with friends, I just didn't feel the same. It was like I wasn't supposed to be there. It was like that little seed was moving around trying to come to life. But, I didn't know how to help it. Something just didn't feel right. It was kinda like I felt something turning on the inside of me to go back to that Cowboy Church and find out more. I would fight this feeling with everything I had. I wasn't going to be a "Church Going Person." Are you crazy? What would people think? I had a reputation to keep, you know?

I was a party girl, and a really good one at that. I had invested many years in this mess that I called my life. I had to uphold the things my father told me that I would be. "You know, I can't let him down." He told me that I would never amount to anything and by gosh that's what I planned on doing. Church, are you nuts? Not this girl! No way!

Chapter 12
The Night I Met Jesus

After I visited the Cowboy Church and listened to Glenn Smith, months had gone by. And one night when I had used way too much "meth" my heart was beating at least 1000 beats per minute, or so it felt. And just a few weeks earlier, I had heard of someone's heart blowing up from this stuff and they had died, so I got a little scared. You see the party was over and I was at home alone in my bed waiting to die, when the words that Cowboy Preacher had been saying came rushing back into my thoughts, "If you want that void filled in your life, then all you have to do is ask Jesus to come live inside your heart." I thought, "Well, it couldn't hurt. My heart needed some kind of help that's for sure."

You see, I was tired and I had lost who I really was. In reality I was broke, I was busted, and totally disgusted with the life I was living. I felt like I had been walking through mud for years, and the mud had totally sucked my boots right off of me. Have you ever felt like that? Like you've been walking in mud and you're so tired that you can't go another step? I felt like I had two left feet and I was walking in circles. I had fallen in the deepest mud pit of my life. I was right back where I was when I was locked up in that basement back in Kansas City. I didn't even know what my life was all about.

I had no direction, no hope and no dreams. I was totally empty inside.

I was living a life that was given to me by my father's words. My father's words were very powerful and they determined the course that I followed. I am not putting all the blame on my father for what happened in my out of control life. It was just like the little girl in the story at the beginning of this book, I had choices and I ended up making the wrong ones over and over.

I never dreamed that I could have a second chance; I had been told and came to believe that this is the only life I could have, so I just had to "deal with it."

You know, all I wanted from day one was a loving family, a warm home with a yard and to hear the sounds of joyous laughter in my home and in my heart. I wanted a home like the Walton's. I would watch the Walton's almost every day, wishing that my life was just like theirs. I just wanted to hear the sounds of laughter and people loving each other. I wanted to hear the sound of a screen door on a hot summer's afternoon and the sound of boots walking on a hard wood floor. I wanted to smell the wonderful smell of coffee in the cool breeze of a winter's morning.

All these things were going on in my head as I laid there in my bed with my heart pounding so fast. I knew that it was time. I knew that I was fixing to die.

So, at that moment, I called out His name. My hero to be, I said, "Jesus" and I paused for a minute – then I said, "If you are really who they say you are, I could use your help. I'm tired of living this life. I'm in need of something real." I am ready to make the trade. I was tired of living a life of pain. I was ready for peace.

I said, "Jesus, can you help me? I don't want to live like this anymore." and that's all I said. And, at that moment, I felt a peace come over me like I had never felt before, and it felt as if someone had sat down beside me, on the edge of my bed. You know, when someone comes and sits on the edge of your bed, how it kinda goes down a little? That's what I felt that night. It was a soft, gentle movement on the side of my bed.

You know, I didn't see angels flying around my room singing praise be to God and the hallelujah song.

I didn't see a bright light shining down from heaven or flashing red lights everywhere. I just felt that small little movement on my bed, like someone had sat down, right next to me. Then at that moment, I felt a warm feeling come over my chest, and my heart started to slow down. With in an hour, I was able to fall off to sleep. That had to have been Jesus, because when Meth overdoses, people do not just fall asleep. I should have been dead or on a lucky non-fatal meth attack, awake for at least five days.

Chapter 13
The Next Morning

Well, I got up the next morning and things really didn't seem too different, or so I thought. I ran to the window to look outside to see if my truck was gone and a bike was in its place. I just knew that a box of Bibles had been delivered to my door with a list of addresses in which to take them.

I just knew that I had "done it," and I was now a "Church Person." No life, no truck, no friends and no brain. Well, there was no bike outside and there was not a box of Bibles. I was very relieved to say the least. I could breathe a little better knowing that I was still in control. So, I went on my way and did what I normally do - BUT, things weren't the same.

45

I didn't seem to have as much fun as before. My desire was different. I couldn't explain, but it was different. I wasn't sure what was going on, but I knew that something had happened that night. So, I went back to that "Cowboy Church" to get some more information on this Jesus person that I had asked to help me. When I walked in I asked the preacher what happened to me. I was for sure that the life I had was done; I am now a "Nerd." Oh No – I'm one of those "Church" people aren't I? The preacher smiled and told me that I had it all wrong. He told me that when I had asked Jesus to come to live in my heart, that I was not the same person as before. I was still me, but not the same bad me. That asking Jesus to come live inside my heart had made me a new person in Him. That everything bad in my life is now gone. I had been forgiven of everything. Everything from that day forward is new and that I had a second chance in life.

He was talking about the life that I had only dreamed of, the one like the Walton's. "Good night John Boys," were in my future! Okay, a little scared of all this, I left not knowing how to handle it. I was unsure of my life and what was in store for me.

I knew that I had to change. Living the way I had was not going to work anymore. I knew deep down inside my spirit that there was a better life for me and I needed to reach out and grab it.

Did you hear what I said? I felt something deep in my spirit. My spirit was finally alive. It wasn't dead anymore. Remember humans are made up of three parts. We consist of a body, soul and spirit. Our bodies contain our five senses and our flesh. The soul is our minds, emotions, and feelings and then there is our spirit, which is dead without the Lord. The spirit is made for the Lord and is dead until you ask Him to come and live there. We are not complete until we have Jesus in our lives. I was now a complete person, but needed to learn how to connect my body and soul to my new living spirit. My mind and emotions were damaged from so many years of wrong thinking and living. I didn't know how to live by my spirit.

I wasn't for sure what to do with it. So the first thing I did after leaving the Church was drive to my drug dealer's home and sit in the driveway for several hours. I didn't know where to go and I didn't know who to call. I had really never been anywhere else. So, I decided to go into my dealer's home and I did one last line with him. Miraculously, the drug didn't have the same affect on my body like they had before. For some reason the feeling I got from it wasn't the same.

I didn't really even like being around these people like before. For some reason, unknown to me at the time, I couldn't get the drug into my body. It wouldn't stay inside. My body would reject it time and time again. It seemed like there was something standing between me and the drugs. Can you guess who? It was Jesus. And before I knew it, I hadn't used in a few weeks. The desire to use had started to leave and I felt better than I ever had. I finally understood the meaning of receiving the gift of a new life in Christ. I needed to learn more about this new me and how to live the life that God had set aside just for me. I needed to learn how to connect my body and soul to my new alive spirit. I needed to get my thinking inline with my spirit, and that alone was a challenge to say the least.

Chapter 14
Restored to Wholeness

You know, I tried to fill that void in my life with drugs, alcohol, men and even money, but nothing worked. I was tired and I had totally lost who I was as a person. I was living a fake life. I was like the little girl in the story. I didn't want to give up the life that I knew, no matter how much green poison it left on me. I gave up everything, my family, my children, and a place to call home, and yes I had even given up any type of victory that could have been in my life. At that moment I didn't fill the huge void deep down inside like I use too. I actually felt good for the first time in my life. I didn't hear the harsh words from my father repeating over and over in my head anymore. I actually thought that my life could change and for the first time ever I was a better person.

I just knew that God must have a purpose for me. I wanted to know more about Him and how to live my life according to His wonderful word. I needed someone in my life that knew God and could teach me how to live one day at a time. But, I didn't trust very many people. I tried going to different churches, seeking answers to my long awaited questions. I just couldn't understand how God could love me, because of all the bad stuff I did.

I didn't really know how to pray, but I did the best I could. I asked God to please send someone to help me know Him better. Then a long-time friend came back into my life, and I knew he was sent to me from God. In 1999, I married my soul mate, the love of my life, Toby Abbott.

Toby was a man sent from God Himself. He had been walking with the Lord for most of his life and knew how to show me the trail to follow in order to grow my love and deepen my relationship with my Lord. Toby's spiritual practices and love for our Lord taught me more about God than anything I could have ever asked for on my own. He knew that I had many problems and needed a lot of unconditional love and tender care. He taught me day by day about the love of our Lord Jesus Christ. He told me that in God's word, there was a scripture there just for me. I couldn't believe that God cared enough about me to give me my own scripture. But, it was true. Knowing that I was addicted to needing approval from others, Toby showed me my very own scripture. It was Jeremiah 1:5, "Before we were born He approved of us." My FATHER approved of me? Yes Me! No, not my earthly father, but my real Father. There was the approval I was seeking for so long. This scripture even goes on to say, "He set me apart" and before I was born, "He loved me." How awesome is that? If He, the God of the whole world approves of me, then I must be someone special. This was something that I had never felt before, being special. I even found another scripture in Ephesians 2:10 – which states "For we are God's masterpiece. He has created us anew in Christ Jesus, so we can do the good things he planned for us long ago." This tells me that I am a masterpiece and not a copy. WOW, now tell me how awesome is that? Special, that's me.

Looking back on my life now, I can't believe how far I've come. My wonderful husband is the Senior Pastor of a Cowboy Church based just outside of Dallas, Texas, and you'll never guess who God has transformed me into. Are you ready? I'm the Co-Pastor. I was ordained in 2004 and became one of those, "Church People." My brain wasn't taken away from me, it's still in the right place, but in much better shape, and believe it or not I still drive a truck.

You know, when Jesus restores, He really restores everything. A few years later, my family was restored. My children back in my life; however, I do not talk or see my father much, he is still very abusive. I do pray for him each and everyday though and through the love of Jesus, I have found a way to forgive him for past hurts. My life has been fully restored, by the precious blood of Jesus. See photos of my family that Jesus restored to me on next page.

Chapter 15
The Pit Is Never Too Deep

The Three Types of Pits

The first is someone else's pit. It's a pit that we didn't mean to get into it, but someone has pushed us in there and we can't get out. My father's words and emotional abuse placed me in my first pit of life.

Deep and dark, this pit started a root that resulted in my decisions to live an out of control life.

The second is the pit we stumble into not meaning to, but we do. I went to Kansas City looking for something different and didn't realize that the something I was chasing was going to place me in the deepest, darkest pit of my life. I was so close to the pit that when I look back, I see myself slipping into hell.

The third is the pit that we just run and jump off into knowing that it's there. There were times that I didn't even care what happened to me and the pit seemed like a place I knew better than anything else. So, I found myself there most of the time. I set my home up in the pit of life.

As deep as it was, it was mine and it was my messed up life, until one day when the walls started falling in on me, and I found myself under so much sorrow that I couldn't breathe anymore.

If you find yourself in one of these pits today, I have great news for you. In God's word found in Isaiah 59:1, God says, "Listen! The Lord's arms are not too weak to save you, nor is His ear too deaf to hear you call."

I thank God every day, that He heard my cry for help. His arms reached down in the deepest, darkest pit of my life and picked me up. He set my feet on solid ground and I am living the life of victory and I'm proud to say that I am Happy, for once in my life. You too can have this same joy and peace. All you have to do is ask Him to come and live in your heart. Just like I did that night.

Let me ask you a question, do you have a void in your life that's deep, deep down inside, and you can't seem to fill it with anything? If so, it's time for you to make that trade.

You know, I once heard another speaker talk about Houdini and how he could "Escape" anything. BUT, his great escape came to an end and so will yours. Nothing on this earth is forever. Only Jesus can fill that void that's in your life. He is the only one that can. He came to Earth as a baby born to a virgin, only to die thirty three and a half years later on a cross to save us from eternal life in Hell. He was buried and three days later, He rose again and is alive today. You know someday you will die and there will be a judgment day for you. You need a Savior to stand with you on that judgment day. Jesus is that Savior that you need. He is the only answer for an eternal life in Heaven. Have you ever asked Him to come into your heart and your life? I'm going to give you the chance today to make Him the Lord of your life and to fill that void that's deep down inside of you. Like the little girl in the story, are you ready to make the right "Choice?"

In the Bible Romans 10:9 tells us that, "If you confess with your mouth that Jesus is Lord and believe in your heart that God raised him from the dead, you will be saved."

There is no sin so horrible, cruel, or unthinkable

and no person so wicked that God cannot forgive and cleanse. The Bible teaches us that God is greater than any sin. Your past behaviors, no matter how bad, cannot and will not prevent you from having a relationship with God through the blood of Jesus.

Even before you were born, God made an unchanging decision to forgive you, knowing your sin beforehand. When Jesus Christ died on the cross, He paid the debt for all sin - past, present and even our future sins - yours included!

The word "Grace" can be defined as favor, or compassion. It is to get what you do not deserve. Your sin deserves judgment and punishment. Nevertheless, because you choose to confess and ask for forgiveness, you will receive grace instead. Each time you sin, grace and forgiveness are available for you; not for you to continue in sin, but to give you the ability to walk away from it and start living the life God intended for you to have.

If you are reading this book right now and feel in your heart you too need to make the trade, I would like to lead you in this simple prayer. You need to pray this prayer from the bottom of your heart. Please bow your head and pray with me. Let's pray together.

Dear Lord, I confess to you that I am a sinner in need of a Savior. I believe that you are the son of God and I ask you to forgive me of my sins and fill this void inside me. I give my life to you today, mold me and lead me in your way. In Jesus name, Amen.

If you just prayed this prayer with me and meant it with your heart, then your name has been written in the Lamb's Book of Life, which is God's big book. So, on that judgment day, you can stand before God and know without a doubt that you have eternal life in Heaven.

Let me add this by saying, you need to make Jesus the Lord over your life. Don't just ask Him to come into your heart as fire insurance. Make Him Lord of your life. You need to get into a Bible teaching church and learn how to connect your body and soul to your newly alive spirit. You need to learn how to deal with your mind and the things you think about. As Joyce Meyer has talked about, "Think about what your thinking about."

Please be patient, you didn't get into your mess overnight and you won't get out of it overnight. It is going to take time. Please just take one day at a time. For God gives us new grace for every day. So use the grace for today and tomorrow's grace will come tomorrow. You to will start to enjoy your new life through Christ Jesus, just as I have done. I am living the live of victory and God is in control; not me.

To end my book I would like to say that my father passed away February 26, 2012, but on February 18th he received Jesus as his personal savior. If you are praying for someone, don't stop. I prayed for years for my father to receive Jesus Christ, it may not be you that gets to lead them to the Lord, but pray that God will send someone to them that can. Keep praying and watch the power of the Lord work.

Thank you for allowing me to share my story with you today and may God richly bless your life.

Paula Abbott